Always By Your Side

A GUIDED JOURNAL
OF 75 TREASURES
FROM DADDY TO SON

This Journal Belongs to

. . . . .

_____

Inspiration

· · · · ·

We always love picking the brains and memories of influential people in our lives, giving us insight into our shared history or a nuanced perspective of the world around us. These journals help create a space for children of all ages to learn from and about their parents in a personal and meaningful way.

Included with the prompts are coloring pages, creative writing areas, and more! This series was inspired by an amazing colleague when we were both youth coordinators for a non-profit. One of the many, many things we loved about her was her open communication and the strong relationships she built the students in the programs as well as with her own children. After she lost her battle with cancer, we considered the unanswered questions her children, and countless others have during momentous occasions, when a loved one passes.

We resolved that when we had children we would strive to have conversations with them to answer these questions. Fast forward to our first child. I began a journal for her when she was born. I wrote about the fun things I observed her doing, the funny things she would say, as well as the conversations I wanted to have with her in the future. Thinking of our friend, I also began to write about topics, events, and experiences our daughter may encounter in the future. Those ideas were compiled into this journal resource to help parents build strong relationships and leave a legacy of wisdom and comfort for their children.

The best
part of
being your
Dad is

Date _____

_____

_____

_____

_____

_____

_____

_____

_____

_____

_____

_____

_____

_____

_____

_____

_____

_____

_____

_____

_____

_____

_____

_____

_____

_____

I *hope you always remember the time when we*

Date_____

_____

_____

_____

_____

_____

_____

_____

_____

_____

_____

_____

_____

_____

_____

_____

_____

*On your
first day
of school*

Date

My parents used to tell me

What I
loved about my
first car was

Date_____

_____
_____
_____

_____
_____
_____
_____
_____
_____
_____
_____
_____
_____
_____
_____
_____
_____
_____
_____
_____
_____
_____
_____
_____

This is how you should handle yourself when you lose or when you win

Date_____

_____

_____

_____

_____

_____

_____

_____

_____

_____

_____

_____

_____

_____

_____

_____

_____

_____

_____

_____

My five
favorite
songs are

Date _____

_____

_____

_____

You need to know this about girls

Date _____

_____

_____

_____

*One person
who has
significantly
influenced my
life is*

Date

When you
were a toddler,
I laughed
hysterically
when you

Date_____

_____

_____

_____

_____

_____

_____

_____

_____

_____

_____

_____

_____

_____

_____

_____

_____

_____

_____

When your body starts to change

Date_____

_____

_____

_____

_____

_____

_____

_____

_____

_____

_____

_____

_____

_____

_____

_____

_____

_____

_____

_____

_____

In school, I
was really
good at

Date_____

_____

_____

_____

_____

_____

_____

_____

_____

_____

_____

_____

_____

_____

_____

_____

_____

_____

_____

_____

_____

Never let
anyone tell
you

Date_____

_____

_____

_____

_____

_____

_____

_____

_____

_____

_____

_____

_____

_____

_____

_____

_____

_____

_____

_____

_____

_____

_____

When in doubt

Date_____

_____

_____

_____

*Some of
my favorite
ways to give
back are*

Date_____

_____

_____

_____

_____

_____

_____

_____

_____

_____

_____

_____

_____

_____

_____

_____

_____

_____

_____

_____

_____

"No" is a complete sentence. "No." always means no and this is what I mean...

Date

Here's a
funny story
from my
childhood

Date _____

When it comes to religion and spirituality, I feel like

Date_____

_____
_____
_____
_____

_____
_____
_____
_____
_____
_____
_____
_____
_____
_____
_____
_____
_____
_____
_____
_____
_____
_____
_____

A
gentleman
should
always

Date _____

_____

_____

_____

_____

_____

_____

_____

_____

_____

_____

_____

_____

_____

_____

_____

_____

_____

_____

_____

_____

_____

Growing up being an only child, youngest child, middle child, or oldest child (circle one) was

Date_____

_____
_____
_____
_____

_____
_____
_____
_____
_____
_____
_____
_____
_____
_____
_____
_____
_____
_____
_____
_____
_____
_____
_____
_____
_____

Now that you're a teenager

Date _____

_____
_____
_____

_____
_____
_____
_____
_____
_____
_____
_____
_____
_____
_____
_____
_____
_____
_____
_____
_____
_____
_____
_____
_____

After high school, I chose to

Date _____

_____
_____
_____

_____
_____
_____
_____
_____
_____
_____
_____
_____
_____
_____
_____
_____
_____
_____
_____
_____
_____
_____
_____
_____

When I am sad,
I do this to make
sure I don't stay
in a sad space for
too long

Date _____

_____

_____

_____

_____

_____

_____

_____

_____

_____

_____

_____

_____

_____

_____

_____

_____

_____

_____

_____

_____

_____

_____

_____

A true
friend will
never

My three
favorite
books are

Date _____

_____

_____

_____

_____

_____

_____

_____

_____

_____

_____

_____

_____

_____

_____

_____

_____

_____

_____

_____

_____

_____

_____

*Your first
co-ed party
by yourself,
remember to*

Date _____

_____

_____

_____

My favorite
vacation
with you
was

Date _____

_____
_____
_____

To me, love looks like

Date _____

_____

_____

_____

When you're ready to ask someone on a date, keep this in mind

Date _____

_____

_____

_____

If I could
have a super
power, it
would be

Date

Is *it time for your*
driver's license
already? Always
remember to

Date _____

_____

_____

_____

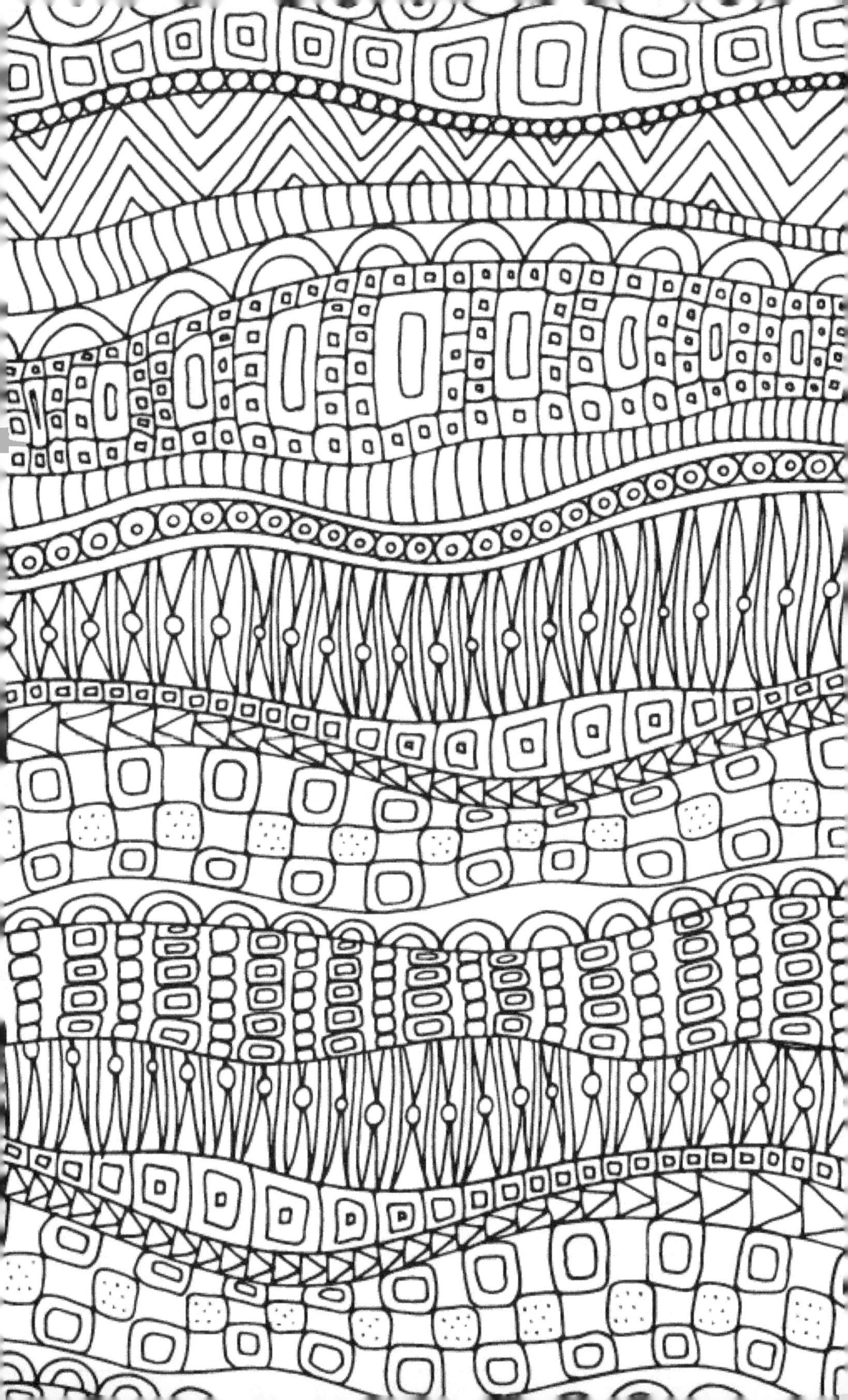

My *two*
favorite
quotes are

Date_____

_____

_____

_____

_____

_____

_____

_____

_____

_____

_____

_____

_____

_____

_____

_____

_____

_____

_____

_____

_____

_____

_____

_____

Growing up,
my favorite
thing to do with
my family was

Date _____

_____

_____

_____

_____

_____

_____

_____

_____

_____

_____

_____

_____

_____

_____

_____

_____

_____

_____

_____

_____

Some things that I learned in school that I actually used in real life

Date_____

_____

_____

_____

_____

_____

_____

_____

_____

_____

_____

_____

_____

_____

_____

_____

_____

_____

_____

_____

_____

_____

_____

A true
friend will
always

Date_____
_____
_____
_____

*On your first
date, I want
you to
remember*

Date_____

_____

_____

_____

_____

_____

_____

_____

_____

_____

_____

_____

_____

_____

_____

_____

_____

_____

I have always enjoyed movies that

What I learned from my first job

Date_____

_____

_____

_____

_____

_____

_____

_____

_____

_____

_____

_____

_____

_____

_____

_____

_____

_____

_____

_____

_____

_____

_____

*On your
prom night,
I want you
to know*

Date _____

_____

_____

_____

Here's an
interesting
story about
your Mom

Date

*Breaking up
usually feels
horrible;
however,*

When I was younger, I remember getting in trouble for

Date_____

_____

_____

_____

_____

_____

_____

_____

_____

_____

_____

_____

_____

_____

_____

_____

_____

_____

_____

_____

_____

_____

_____

Traits you should value in the person you'd want to be your significant other

Date_____

_____

_____

_____

_____

_____

_____

_____

_____

_____

_____

_____

_____

_____

_____

_____

_____

_____

_____

_____

_____

_____

_____

When you
ride a bus
or a plane,
remember to

Date

I look at
you with
wonder and
amazement that

Date_____

_____
_____
_____

Here are a
few tips to
nail that
interview

Date _____

Growing up,
my siblings
and I used to

Date_____

_____

_____

_____

_____

_____

_____

_____

_____

_____

_____

_____

_____

_____

_____

_____

_____

_____

_____

_____

_____

_____

Here are my
definitions for
"failure" and
"success"

Date

_____

_____

_____

_____

You know
you've
found true
love when

Date_____

_____

_____

_____

_____

_____

_____

_____

_____

_____

_____

_____

_____

_____

_____

_____

_____

_____

_____

_____

_____

One thing that
used to bother
and doesn't
anymore is

Date

On the day of your graduation

Date _____

_____

_____

_____

_____

_____

_____

_____

_____

_____

_____

_____

_____

_____

_____

_____

_____

_____

_____

_____

_____

Some things that life taught me that I never learned in school

Date _____

_____

_____

_____

_____

_____

_____

_____

_____

_____

_____

_____

_____

_____

_____

_____

_____

_____

_____

_____

_____

_____

_____

*Communicating
with the parents
of someone you "like"
can be tricky, but*

Date _____

_____

_____

_____

_____

The first time I lived on my own, I

I've
always
dreamed of

*On your
wedding day,
I want you
to know*

Date

My
favorite
place to
visit is

Date

Self-care is important. Here are some ways I enjoy practicing self-care.

Date _____

_____

_____

_____

I would use these three powerful adjectives to describe you

Date_____

_____

_____

_____

_____

_____

_____

_____

_____

_____

_____

_____

_____

_____

_____

_____

_____

_____

_____

_____

Here's the
secret
recipe to

Date _____

_____

_____

_____

_____

_____

_____

_____

_____

_____

_____

_____

_____

_____

_____

_____

_____

_____

_____

_____

_____

_____

_____

On your
wedding night,
make sure you
consider

Date

*If you ever
feel down on
your luck,
remember*

Date

No matter how wealthy you become, always remember

Date_____

_____

_____

_____

_____

_____

_____

_____

_____

_____

_____

_____

_____

_____

_____

_____

_____

_____

_____

_____

_____

I *remember*
the time
you

Date_____

_____

_____

_____

_____

_____

_____

_____

_____

_____

_____

_____

_____

_____

_____

_____

_____

_____

_____

_____

_____

_____

_____

_____

*On your
journey to
becoming wise,
remember to*

Date

*Celebrating the
birth of your
baby, I want
you to know*

Date _____

_____

_____

_____

_____

_____

_____

_____

_____

_____

_____

_____

_____

_____

_____

_____

_____

_____

_____

_____

_____

_____

_____

_____

Did you know I used to

Date_____

_____

_____

_____

_____

_____

_____

_____

_____

_____

_____

_____

_____

_____

_____

_____

_____

_____

_____

_____

_____

_____

_____

_____

Everybody
makes mistakes.
When you
mess up

Now that you're a Dad

Date _____

_____
_____
_____

I *love this*
about you

Date_____

_____

_____

_____

_____

_____

_____

_____

_____

_____

_____

_____

_____

_____

_____

_____

_____

_____

_____

_____

_____

_____

_____

_____

*Above all
else, always
remember*

A few things
every man
should learn
how to do

Date

Some favorite memories I have of my grandparents

Date _____

_____

_____

_____

_____

_____

_____

_____

_____

_____

_____

_____

_____

_____

_____

_____

_____

_____

_____

_____

_____

_____

_____

Dont' be
afraid to

Date

As a grown-up,
my favorite
thing to do with
my family is

Date _____

_____

_____

_____

_____

_____

_____

_____

_____

_____

_____

_____

_____

_____

_____

_____

_____

_____

_____

_____

_____

I want you to always know how proud I am of you and

Date _____

_____

_____

_____

_____

_____

_____

_____

_____

_____

_____

_____

_____

_____

_____

_____

_____

_____

_____

_____

_____

_____

Free Write

.....

Now that you've got the hang of it, use the following pages to write about topics more specific to you and your family, go into more detail about something previously discussed, or let your son ask you some questions that have sparked his curiosity.

Date

Date

Date_____

Date_____

Date

Date_____

Date_____

Date

Date

Date_____

Family Tree

On the next page, you can map out your family tree. Use the circles to write your family members' names and use the lines to write how they are related to you. See the example below for an idea of how to complete your own. There's no right or wrong way. Have fun! Be creative!

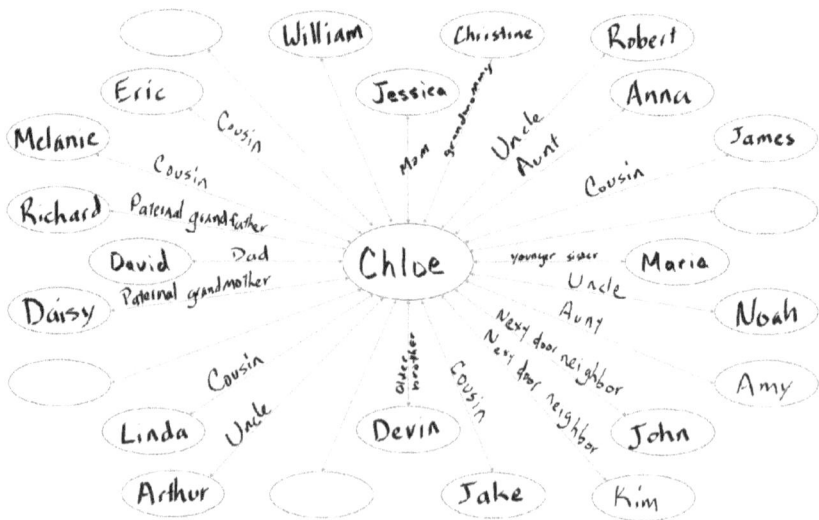

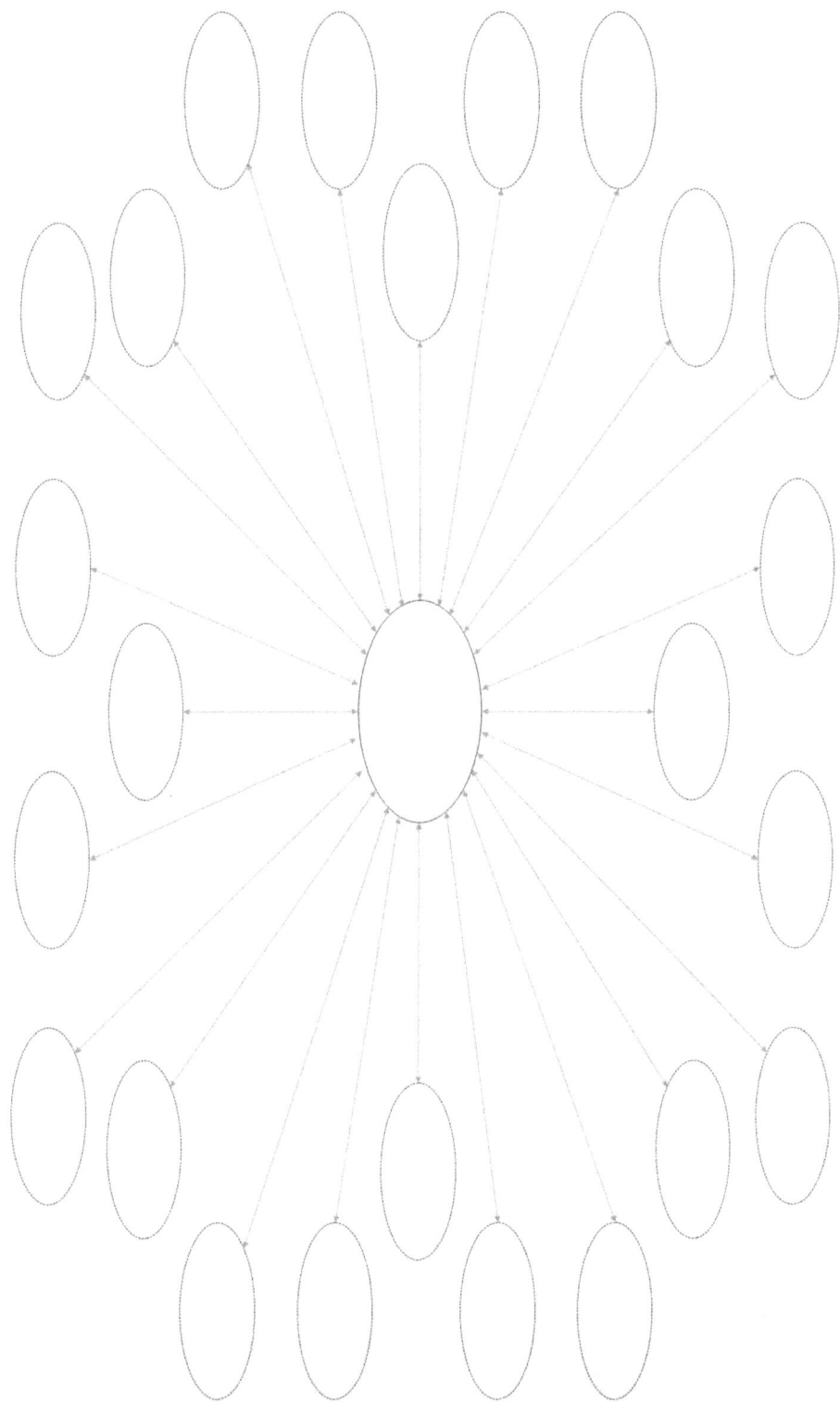

You and Me

· · · · ·

Full Name   Full Name

Birthdate   Birthdate

Birth Weight   Birth Weight

Picture of Us